The Sparrow

The Sparrow

Written and illustrated by
Kathy Nelton

For the lost pets
and the people who love them.

The author with Lance

The Sparrow

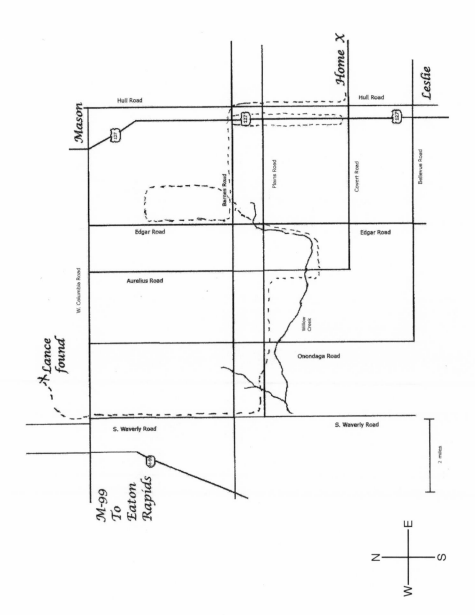

1

As I rushed to put the horses in for the night, gun shots rang out in the distance. It was the first day of deer season and the hunters were out in full force. I was trying to catch the horses, but Sweetie, the fiery red-and-white pinto, was giving me some trouble. The gunfire had made her flighty, but in the end a handful of grain solved the problem and she was soon safe in her stall.

I had left the dogs outside to run in the yard as I finished my barn chores. As I came around the side of the house, they ran to greet me. They bounced around, barking wildly, but despite the chaos, it only took a moment to realize that Lance was not among them.

Lance had been born at our house four years earlier. He was a large sheltie with a lovely, profuse silvery coat. His temperament could only be described as sweet. Calm, quiet and devoted, he was one of my favorites. To run like this was not at all like him.

Hastily, I put the remaining dogs in the house and ran as fast as I could down the road toward the apple orchard at the top of the hill. The brisk wind tossed snow flurries around me as I raced between the barren trees calling his name.

I caught a fleeting glimpse of Lance as he entered the yard of the house nearest the orchard. I tried to follow, but a large Rottweiler blocked my path. Its presence and bark were ominous enough to warrant my retreat.

I was not ready to give up. I walked along the road, frantically calling his name. However, as the sun set, it became clear that it was best to resume my search in the morning.

The next day I printed "Lost Dog" posters, and the arduous task of going door-to-door to speak to anyone who might have seen him began. Saturday came to an end yielding no results. However, Sunday morning brought a glimmer of hope as the day broke with a phone call. A man called to inform us that he had seen Lance near the trailer park three miles away. Encouraged, my husband and I drove to a nearby field where we found the man waiting for us. We looked off into the distance, and about 150 feet away at the edge of a woods stood Lance. I called to him and began to approach, but he turned to run. My heart sank. Had he literally become a wild animal? Had he lost all memory of me?

The following weekend was Thanksgiving. During that time we received a call from my friend Andrea. Her sister had sighted Lance in the darkness of night, running down our local expressway US-127. For the entire four day weekend I drove that stretch of busy highway without a glimpse of him. Finally I decided that we should lure him off the highway by making a trail of hot dogs to the exit. The delectable trail was carefully laid along the shoulder of the highway. As I jogged along the busy road, I noticed bemused expressions on the faces of people passing by. Some motorists must have been greatly perplexed by the sight of a woman tossing hot dogs behind her as she ran toward the exit.

On Sunday night at 10pm the phone rang. To my surprise, the sheriff's department was calling to inform me that two deputies had seen Lance near the expressway exit on Barnes Road. I was touched by their kindness. Earlier, I had placed a poster on their bulletin board in the hope that someone on road patrols might spot my prodigal canine. After the phone call, I drove to the spot and saw a solitary canine figure walking along the dark, lonely road. It was Lance. I pulled the car over and slowly opened the door. Mesmerized, he stood there, his eyes reflecting the headlights' bright glare. Gently tossing some pieces of hot dog toward him, I spoke his name softly, hoping that he would remember me. It was fruitless. Within seconds, he was off and running again, and he quickly disappeared into the night.

2

The week following Thanksgiving brought more frustration and disappointment. On Monday, my daughter Kris accompanied me to the local dog pound. We placed a poster on the bulletin board, then went to the window where an employee took my driver's license and signed us in. She buzzed the door open and we walked into the cinder block kennel amidst the sound of exuberant barking.

As we walked down the aisle, I was moved by the sight of the unfortunate wards of the county. Among them we saw many large dogs, mostly mixed breeds and Labs. The younger dogs bounded against the chain link kennels and barked loudly. Most of the older dogs sat pensively, resigned to accept the sad fate that awaited most of them. I most clearly remember the sight of two old beagles, shaking and looking as though they hadn't a friend left in the world. They sat cowering in the corner of their kennel and their eyes reflected the profound sadness they must have felt, realizing that they were victims of the ultimate betrayal. I couldn't help but feel compassion for them and their great misfortune of being abandoned by some heartless owner.

We passed kennel after kennel and saw every size and shape of dogs but we did not find Lance among them.

Shortly after we arrived home the phone rang. A stranger called to tell us that a collie-like dog was lying dead on the median of US-127. I thanked them, and with dread in my heart I drove to the site. The dog I found there was indeed a small collie or a very large sheltie. The coat was so dirty and matted that the color was nearly impossible to distinguish. After gazing at the unfortunate dog for several minutes I determined that it was not my Lance. In walking back to my car conflicting thoughts raced through my mind. As much as I wanted to find him alive, in a way, it would have been a relief if it *had* been him. To not know what was happening to him was tearing me apart.

Several days passed and after giving it much thought, I decided that my best course of action would be to rent a live trap.

After renting the trap, I continued to talk to people and place flyers in newspaper boxes. Eventually I arrived at the home of the Horns, who I later discovered were friends of Andrea. When I explained my situation to Mrs. Horn, she was sympathetic (she owned Shelties as well) and allowed me to place a live trap on their property. Lance had been seen in the area, and I felt that there was a good chance that his desire for food could lure him into a trap. The trap was set and for the first time in many days, I felt optimistic.

However, it wasn't long before the feelings of optimism faded. A few days later I received a call from Mrs. Horn informing me that unfortunately the only things being caught in the trap were opossums and feral cats. Disappointed, I drove to her home to pick up the trap and return it to the dog pound.

3

Our days followed the same pattern, running together into an unending nightmare. I home-schooled my younger daughter Kristin, and her older sister Bre attended public school. After Bre went off to school, Kris and I began our lessons. At noon for an hour or two we drove the country roads placing more flyers into the newspaper boxes of rural residents.

The task was daunting, but this period of time proved to be quite fruitful. We received many calls from people who had seen Lance. I ran the ad with his photo in our local shopping guide week after week, hoping that by keeping his photo public we would have a greater chance of bringing him home.

Several people were very helpful and offered to keep food out for him. Others called me more than once as he often stayed in the same area for many days. Their patience and compassion were overwhelming and I knew that there was no way that I could ever repay their kindness. One evening we were resting quietly at home, when the peace was shattered by the ringing of the phone. The caller was a lady who had seen him on more than one occasion. He had been there moments before, and she advised me to come right away. It was late and my eyes were heavy as I drove the dark, winding country roads.

When I arrived, I knocked on her door. She opened it and invited me inside. She proceeded to tell me that he was in her yard prior to my arrival, but had just taken off down the road.

She pointed the way and I began to walk into the blackness of the night, with flash light in hand, calling his name, and pitching hot dogs into the drainage ditch that ran along the side of the road. There was a full moon, and the trees cast eerie shadows against the moonlit snow. I came to a spot on the road near a decrepit house. It was in a state of disrepair and a myriad of disabled vehicles littered the yard. A bad feeling came over me, and suddenly I felt fear for the first time at being alone out on a dark country road. My cowardice got the best of me, and I gave up my search for the night.

In the following weeks I must have encountered at least twenty people who had seen him. All of them helped as much as they could. One farmer told me that, although he would continue to watch for my dog, Lance was in great danger, not only from hunters who wouldn't hesitate to shoot a dog suspected of chasing deer, but also the coyotes that lived in the woods and fields. I appreciated his candor, but it was the last thing that I wanted to hear.

The reports continued. Lance had been seen throughout the neighboring countryside. In spite of the bitter cold, it was actually the best time for him to be lost. Due to the lack of vegetation he was easily seen and the snow made it easy to track him. The deer were in rut, which led to many of them getting hit by cars. It was indeed a blessing in disguise, because he was often seen near deer carcasses which offered him a source of badly needed sustenance.

I often wondered what kept me going as I walked the woods and fields during those weeks of bitter cold. Maybe it was my love for Lance. Maybe it was my dedication to the memory of his mother who perished tragically in a house fire the year before. No matter what the reason, I was not about to give up on him no matter how hopeless the situation appeared.

4

The time between Thanksgiving and Christmas passed quickly and before we knew it, Christmas Eve was upon us. Everyone was gathered at my parents' house for the holiday celebration. As the conversation flowed and the sound of children's laughter filled the air, my mind drifted to thoughts of Lance. I wondered if he was cold, hungry or thirsty. So far, the winter had been very bleak and bitterly cold. Even in this season of cheer and goodwill, it was difficult to get lost in the festivities. He continued to haunt my thoughts.

We enjoyed a wonderful dinner of roasted turkey with all of the trimmings. After the table was cleared we went into the living room to open gifts. I loved watching my daughters open their presents, and as the evening progressed, I was able to forget the sorrow and frustration of the previous weeks. A warm glow filled the room and the love of family temporarily overcame my grief.

While we were preparing to leave, my mother offered to give us some leftovers to take home. I gladly accepted and after saying our good-byes we were on our way.

As we drove I gazed out of the car window over the bleak landscape, and my thoughts drifted to Lance. I asked my husband Bill if we could stop at the field where he was last seen and drop off the leftovers. We drove down the dark, tree-lined country roads until we reached our destination. As I got out of the car and trudged through the deep snow, delicate snow flakes gently drifted through the air. An oppressive pall of silence filled the atmosphere and the only thing I heard was the crunching of the snow beneath my feet. I carefully set the plastic containers down in the snow. As I turned to go back to the car, I prayed that Lance would discover the turkey and gravy which would hopefully offer some respite from his hunger.

Within a half hour we arrived home. The car lights illuminated the barn as we pulled into our driveway. We unloaded the car and went into the dark house. The girls got ready for bed, and as I tucked them in, I had a deep sense of how blessed I really was. Family and the love it brings is everything. Their innocent play always filled my heart with laughter. They were such a blessing in this time of worry and loss. We said our prayers and I kissed them goodnight. As I turned out the light and closed the door, I prayed that the Lord would guide and protect my Lance.

5

The time between Christmas and the New Year was very relaxed. The girls played with their Christmas gifts and enjoyed their time off from school. I savored the time I had with them during the holidays. We could just have fun, with no schedules to meet or homework to do. The week passed quickly. In spite of the girls' non-stop imaginary play with stuffed toys or dolls, we still found time to spend in our search for Lance. We continued the long drives along snow covered country roads and weekly visits to the animal shelter. The last week had brought no responses from our newspaper ad. Previously, the phone had rung at least three or four times a week, but the period between Christmas and New Years yielded no new sightings of my dog.

The early afternoon of New Year's Eve brought a phone call from Annette. Annette was a friend I hadn't heard from in over a year. It was nice to talk with her. We chatted briefly and then she told me the reason for her call. She had found a lost dog, and she wanted my veterinarian's phone number to see if they could check their bulletin board for potential matches. I told her of Lance's disappearance and she replied that she would watch for him. I politely thanked her, but I was skeptical. Annette lived fifteen miles west of us. Previous sightings placed Lance traveling in a circle going north and south. The possibility of them crossing paths seemed quite remote.

New Years Eve was spent at home with the girls. From the living room their laughter drifted with the sounds of the television and gave me a sense of normalcy. I let them stay up until midnight to welcome in the New Year, then we all went to bed, unaware of what the next day would bring.

On New Years Day, the afternoon brought a welcome call from a woman who had seen Lance. She told me that her neighbor had gone out on his snowmobile with a rifle, searching for coyotes. As he approached the crest of the hill, he spotted what he thought was a wild canine entangled in a barbed wire fence. Moving closer, he realized that the dog was a sheltie and quickly sped off to her house. Since she had shelties, he was concerned that it might be one of her dogs.

They both trudged to the top of the hill but as they approached, Lance panicked and using every last ounce of strength broke free from the barbed wire that imprisoned him. They stood there, watching helplessly as he disappeared into the neighboring woods.

She then remembered seeing our ad and returned to her house to call me. I asked if I could come over and she said yes. I quickly grabbed my coat, jumped into the car and soon arrived at her farm which was just a couple miles away. As I got out of my car, she greeted me and we both walked across the barren field and up the hill to the spot where Lance was last seen. The barbed wire still held fragments of his silver blue hair. I looked to my right and just beyond a fence were the woods that he vanished into. As I approached the fence, I saw a cage holding a dead coyote. Its mouth gaped open in a macabre silent scream. I asked the woman if the property belonged to her. She told me that it belonged to some undesirable types and that the acreage was laced with steel jaw leg hold traps. With the revelation of that dreadful news, my heart sank. So far Lance had survived many dangers, but this seemed most foreboding.

Depression engulfed me for the remainder of the week. I felt my strength draining and wondered how much longer I could keep up this apparently futile effort. In spite of the increasing hopelessness, something compelled me to keep going.

The weekend brought the renewing church services that my

spirit so desperately needed. After the service Mrs. Howard asked me how my search was progressing and told me that she was continuing to pray for Lance's return. I thanked her and felt encouraged knowing that at least one person continued to bring my petition before the Lord.

After church I returned to the field where he was last seen. As I climbed the steep snow covered hill, the strong bitter wind stung my face. The tears began to flow and burned my cheeks, as I looked over the bleak, vast landscape. As the overwhelming hopelessness of the situation engulfed me I cried out to God. Submerged in a sea of despair, I told Him that I was ending my search and turning it all over to Him. If Lance was going to come home, the only thing that could bring him was the Hand of God.

Completely surrendered, I turned to go home. The wind howled as I slowly descended the hill. As the snow crunched beneath my feet, I felt a strange peace envelop me as I placed my faith in the Great Creator.

6

Totally exhausted, I went to bed early. My slumber brought a very strange dream whose meaning was not apparent at first. The location of my dream was a place called Willow Creek. I had never heard of this place before, but in the dream I was told to follow it in order to find Lance. In the vision, I did search this area but did not find him. The first thing I did when I awoke was go to my husband's atlas, and amazingly there was a Willow Creek that ran west along Plains Road toward Eaton Rapids.

Tuesday brought a call from my friend Andrea. She told me that when they were returning home from a 4-H meeting, suddenly her daughter Lauren said, "Stop the car. I think Lance is here." Andrea laughed and told Lauren that it was too dark to search and they proceeded home. I asked her where they were when this happened, and she replied that they were on Plains Road.

I *knew* that something was beginning to happen, and for the first time in many weeks, I felt encouraged.

The following day, Annette called to inform me that she spotted Lance on Columbia Road near her home, while she was on her way to the vet in Mason. I was skeptical as she lived near Eaton Rapids, so I naturally asked her where she had seen him. She said it was near the golf course, which I knew was just north of Willow Creek. Feeling a glimmer of hope, I told her that I would be right over with a photo of Lance. When I arrived, she confirmed that the dog she saw was indeed Lance. We jumped into my car, and drove around the neighboring streets until we saw a man shoveling snow. I got out of the car and asked him if he had seen a lost sheltie. I showed him a photo of Lance, and he confirmed that he did see my dog. He pointed across the road to a field adjacent to the golf course. I thanked him, and we returned to the car. We drove across the road to another house and asked for permission to continue our search on their property. The lady was very kind and agreed to let us look for Lance. We searched for around an hour. It was getting dark and our efforts had yielded nothing. Crestfallen, I returned home.

Later that evening, Annette received a call from the woman saying that Lance was on her property. Annette had gone there, but he had vanished by the time she arrived. I warned them both not to chase him for fear that he would leave the area. We were so close to capturing him, and I did not want to jeopardize his safe return.

My husband returned from work with some tranquilizers that he picked up from our vet. My plan was to lace some meat with the drugs, and hopefully slow Lance down enough to ensure his capture.

The next morning I picked up Annette and once again we began our search. It was a gray, overcast morning. A strange calm filled the air as we walked across the snow covered field. Our trek led us to a winding frozen creek, and we decided to follow the icy trail to see where it would lead us. The creek was flanked by towering, tree-covered banks that rose high above us on either side. My heart pounded wildly with anticipation at the thought that my long search might finally be nearing an end. As we rounded the bend Annette looked up and pointed. "There he is," she exclaimed. My gaze slowly rose to the crest of the bank where he stood looking down upon us. Slowly, I ascended the steep, snow-covered creek bank. The tension of those moments overwhelmed me and made the climb seem to last an eternity. Once I reached the summit, I was around fifteen feet from Lance. Slowly kneeling, I gently spoke to him. His eyes were filled with growing anxiety, and it was very apparent that he still didn't recognize me. His body stiffened, and he looked as if he was ready to bolt. I slowly inched toward him, but with each advance, his panic intensified, his eyes reflecting ever-increasing fear. My mind traveled back to the despair and hopelessness that hounded me for the last two months. The days filled with hours of frantic searching, the disappointments, and not knowing whether he was dead or alive. Finally, he was almost within my reach but within seconds could be so far away. The anguish I felt at the possibility of losing him again was consuming. I could no longer endure the stress, and the emotion of that moment overwhelmed me. I burst into tears, pleading to my dear dog to come to me. In that instant, a deafening silence enveloped us. For a brief moment, time seemed to stand still as the stark quiet of that cold winter morning filled the air. Slowly, he turned toward me. His body began to relax. The fear left his eyes, and his tail slowly wagged. As I knelt there sobbing, he trotted toward me, and gazing tenderly into my eyes, he gently licked my face. My arms quickly enveloped him, and at that moment the great burden that I carried for so many weeks immediately dissipated. Thanking and praising God, I held Lance tightly as he licked away my tears. Greatly relieved, I scooped him up in my arms, and Annette and I trudged through the deep snow to the car. My long search had finally ended. We both cried tears of joy, realizing that we had just been a part of an amazing miracle.

7

Amazingly, despite being gone for almost two months, Lance was in excellent health. He had lost no weight and only had some burrs and sore feet to show for his great adventure.

From then on we kept our gate closed, in hope of preventing a repeat performance of his escape.

A few days after his return, there was a knock at the door. It was Mrs. Horn. She smiled as she handed me a bag of dog treats. Attached to the bag were a bright red bow and a note. The note read:

Dear Lance,

You are one special dog. Your mom loves you so much that she spent many weeks looking for you and never gave up. Many people were praying for you as well. Then at the time when things looked the most hopeless, God used you to show us all that He cares even for the littlest sparrow.

I read the note and smiled. What she said was true. The good Lord had indeed used a humble dog to show us all that miracles still exist and that He is there to help us, if we will only let Him.

Epilogue

Lance went on to live to be eleven years old. He passed away in March of 2002. We've had other dogs since his passing, but he still holds a special place in my heart.

I've written this book to the glory of God and the miracles that He performs every day in the lives of people all over the world. Like me, so many people become overwhelmed with their situation, losing sight of God's love and desire to play an active role in our lives. My own situation was seemingly impossible as Lance in his blinding fear met with the danger of being on a major interstate for four days and faced hunters, steel jaw leg-hold traps, starvation, thirst, cold, and coyotes. I looked for Lance and prayed for him every day for nearly two months, but it wasn't until I turned everything over to God that within four days my dog was placed safely within my arms. I feel that God gave me this experience in order to encourage others to surrender their problems to Him and to believe that miraculous outcomes can spring even from the most hopeless situations.

It is my prayer that this story has strengthened your faith and given you renewed assurance that, even in the darkest moments of your life, God is always with you.

Made in the USA
Coppell, TX
11 July 2022

79800403R00025